1 MONTH OF FREE READING

at

www.ForgottenBooks.com

By purchasing this book you are eligible for one month membership to ForgottenBooks.com, giving you unlimited access to our entire collection of over 1,000,000 titles via our web site and mobile apps.

To claim your free month visit:
www.forgottenbooks.com/free715242

ISBN 978-0-666-36637-5
PIBN 10715242

:ON BULLETIN 525
April, 1983

SOD SEEDING OF FORAGES
Alternative to Conventional Establishment

by

D.W. Koch, G.W. Mueller-Warrant, and J.R. Mitchell

NEW HAMPSHIRE
AGRICULTURAL EXPERIMENT STATION
UNIVERSITY OF NEW HAMPSHIRE
DURHAM, NEW HAMPSHIRE 03824

ISSN: 0077-8338

ON BULLETIN 525   April, 1983

SOD SEEDING OF FORAGES
Alternative to Conventional Establishment

by

D.W. Koch, G.W. Mueller-Warrant, and J.R. Mitchell

NEW HAMPSHIRE
AGRICULTURAL EXPERIMENT STATION
UNIVERSITY OF NEW HAMPSHIRE
DURHAM, NEW HAMPSHIRE 03824

ACKNOWLEDGEMENTS

The authors wish to thank Stephen Bunker, Kingman Farm
Superintendent, for his assistance in conducting the trials and
Monsanto Co., Chevron Chemical Co., and Rhom and Haas Co. for
supplying herbicides used in the trials.

ABSTRACT

The potential of seeding directly into sod as an alternative to the conventional preparation of a fine seedbed was investigated. Several seedings involving alfalfa, red clover, birdsfoot trefoil, timothy, and orchardgrass were made in 1976-77 on. three different soils. Both conventional and sod seedings generally increased legume, forage and protein yields. Seedling growth and development were slower following sod seeding and yields were lower than those from conventional seeding the year of establishment. In the year following seeding, however, yields from sod and conventional seedings were similar, considering the highest yielding treatments of each. With August seeding on a seasonally'wet soil, red clover seeded into sod overwintered successfully, while red clover seeded conventionally failed due to severe heaving. Herbicides were more essential for sod seeding than for conventional seeding, especially with perennial grasses such as quackgrass. Annual weeds were more common with conventional seedings than with sod seedings. Early May seedings of alfalfa were superior to later seedings with both methods of establishment.

KEY WORDS: No Till Seeding, Reduced Tillage, Forage Legume Establishment, Forage Renovation, Forage Grass Establishment.

Table of Contents

ii

SOD SEEDING OF FORAGES

I. Alternative to Conventional Establishment

by

D. W. Koch, G. W. Mueller-Warrant, and J. R. Mitchell[1]

INTRODUCTION

The history of agriculture has been closely linked to tillage of the
soil. Tillage is the term that has been used to describe, collectively,
the operations of plowing, discing, harrowing and dragging to prepare a
fine, firm, clod-free seedbed.

Can we eliminate tillage entirely? First, it is necessary to take a
close look at the need to plow, since most subsequent tillage operations are
necessitated by plowing. A number of reasons can be offered: (1) Plowing
provides a means of burying, and thereby killing, live weedy plants.
(2) Plowing incorporates surface mulch which would interfere with planting,
particularly the ability to obtain good seed-soil contact of small-seeded
forages. (3) Plowing and subsequent tillage provides a means to effectively
adjust soil pH and fertility. (4) Plowing often loosens the soil and may,
on some soils and in some situations, such as on compacted soils, increase
water infiltration, and (5) Incorporation of trash is considered to be a
good sanitary measure for control or prevention of insects and diseases.
These principles have been taught to generations of agronomists and yet
today we consider the total elimination of tillage.

Great strides have been made in recent years toward reducing the need
for tillage. Specialized equipment, known as no-till seeders, are capable
of clearing or penetrating surface trash, preparing a narrow strip seedbed

[1] Associate Professor, former Graduate Research Assistant, and Associate Pro-
fessor, respectively, Plant Science Department, University of New Hampshire,
Durham, N. H. 03824. Mueller-Warrant is currently Assistant Professor,
South Central Kansas Experimental Field, Route 2, Hutchinson, KS 67501.

and precise placement of seed without energy-expensive tillage and labor-intensive operations of preparing a suitable seedbed. Recently herbicides which suppress or kill vegetation and allow seeding into previously live sod without residual toxicity to introduced seedlings have come on the market

Maintaining the killed sod and surface mulch aids in water penetration, minimizes the amount of water running off, and greatly reduces the erosion effect of runoff water and wind. Plant nutrients, seed and pesticides carried in runoff are therefore greatly reduced.

Seeding directly into sod is an attractive alternative to conventional methods of forage establishment in the Northeast where there is a preponderance of hilly, rocky fields and it is either impractical or conservationally unwise to plow and prepare a fitted seedbed.

Much of the forage-producing land in the Northeast sustains very low levels of production due to the presence of unproductive species. Since these species fail to respond adequately to fertility, the lack of liming and fertilization, combined with relatively high rainfall, has led to acidic soils low in plant-available nutrients. Because of the difficulty, time, labor, expense, and lack of technology for introducing improved species, these fields have not been improved.

The purpose of this study was to determine the potential of establishing perennial forages, primarily legumes, directly into sod in relation to conventional seeding.

LITERATURE REVIEW

Some of the earliest work on reducing tillage in relation to renovating non-plowable permanent pastures was conducted by Sprague (1952, 1960). Establishment of orchardgrass and Ladino clover was equally successful with only two discings of a chemically-killed sod as with 10-12 discings, which was considered necessary for preparing a conventional seedbed. A mixture of amitrole and dalapon, applied to a closely grazed sward, effectively killed bluegrass, poverty grass, sweet vernalgrass, and many perennial broadleaf species.

More recently, the availability of non-selective herbicides has improved the control of sod competition, especially competitive weedy species, without residual effect on introduced seedlings. Triplett, et al. (1975) summarized the work of several researchers who have effectively changed the composition of pasture swards with such materials. Other workers have attempted to reduce competition from existing species in order to favor conditions for introduced species (Cullen, 1970; Newman, 1966; and White, 1970). Herbicide use has improved the reliability of no-till legume establishment (Linscott, 1979; Mueller-Warrant and Koch, 1979).

The development of specialized equipment with the capability of placing small-seeded forages in contact with soil without burying surface mulch or residues from previous crops has provided new opportunities (Decker, et al., 1964; Decker, et al., 1969; Taylor, et al., 1969). Forage species which are more responsive to fertility and which are higher in quality than those of the previously existing sod were introduced and with less time, labor and energy than with tilled seedbeds.

Most fields in the Northeast which have not been renovated in a number of years will be largely devoid of legumes. The benefit of introducing legumes to improve productivity has been demonstrated many times. For instance, Wedin et al. (1965) reported that yields of mixtures with 30-40% legumes were equivalent to pure grass stands heavily fertilized with nitrogen.

METHODS AND MATERIALS

Renovation methods

Conventional establishment involved plowing, discing several times, rock removal, firming of seedbed and seeding with a Brillion[1] seeder. Sod seeding involved the use of a John Deere Powrtill[1] drill, equipped with powered coulters which tilled a one-half inch wide strip every 8 inches. There were no tillage operations preceding sod seedings. The herbicide used depended on the sod species present. At all sites the grass was mowed so that a maximum growth of four inches was present at seeding.

Since legumes were seeded in all the studies, no nitrogen was applied before or after seeding, except in Experiment·1, in which nitrogen was applied, along with other fertilizer elements at various rates. To avoid insect damage to new seedlings, Furadan[1] 10G was broadcast at 10 lbs/acre on all plots following seeding.

Table 1 shows the soil and vegetative characteristics of the sites used in the study. Seedings were made in 1976-77 at the Agricultural Experiment Station, Kingman Farm, Madbury, N. H.

Red clover establishment

This experiment was on a Buxton silt loam (Site No. 1, Table 1). It is characterized as a deep soil with layers of clay in the profile which impede vertical water movement and create seasonally high water tables, averaging 16 inches from the surface. Because of high water retention, the soil is prone to heaving and legumes such as alfalfa have poor survival.

---

[1]Mention of a commercial product is for the benefit of the reader and does not imply endorsement by the N.H. Agricultural Experiment Station.

Table 1. Characteristics of experimental sites and treatment variables.

| Site No. | Soil Series | Drainage | Soil fertility | | | Sod Species[a] | Species Seeded | Experimental Variables |
			pH	P	K			
1	Buxton silt loam	Imperfect	5.4	Low	V.low	Quackgrass, broadleaf weeds, timothy, clovers	Red clover-timothy mixture	Seeding methods, seeding dates, fertilizer rates, perennial grass control
2	Hollis-Charlton fine sandy loam	Excessive	5.6	Low	Low	Field brome, red sorrel, hawkweed	Alfalfa-orchardgrass; birdsfoot trefoil-timothy	Seeding methods, forage mixtures
3	Charlton fine sandy loam	Well-drained	6.1	V.high	High	Quackgrass, dandelions	Alfalfa	Seeding methods, seeding dates

[a]Listed in order of presence just prior to renovation.

Dolomitic lime at 1½ tons/acre was applied to the site on June 30 and on August 9, 1976. Conventionally seeded plots were plowed July 9, 1976. so that half the lime was plowed down and half disced into the seedbed.

The field on which this experiment was located (Site No. 1) was seeded 10 years prior to red clover and timothy (Table 1). In July, 1976, quackgrass represented 36%, broadleaf weeds 29%, timothy 25% and clovers 10% of the undisturbed sod. On August 3, 1976, 2,4-D was applied to the entire area at one lb. a.e./acre for control of dandelions and other broadleaf weeds. Sod-seeded plots were mowed four days before seeding and paraquat at one quart/acre with 1% v/v surfactant was applied one day before seeding. All plots were seeded on August 16, 1976, and on May 6, 1977, with a mixture of 12 lbs/acre of 'Pennscott' red clover and 6 lbs/acre of 'Climax' timothy. Paraquat at the rate previously used was applied on May 11 to plots sod-seeded in the spring.

At this site a split block design was used. It was replicated four times with main plots consisting of conventional and sod seedings in August, 1976 and May, 1977, and an unseeded sod control. Subplots consisted of rates of 5-20-20 (none, 250, 500, and 1,000 lbs/acre). Fertilizer was disced into plowed seedbeds, but left on the surface with sod seedings. Sub-subplots were either untreated or treated on November 8, 1976, with Kerb[1] at 1½ lbs a.i./acre.

Establishment of legume-grass mixtures

The Hollis-Charlton soil on which this experiment was located (Site No. 2) is considered to be well to excessively drained and droughty, due to low moisture retention (Table 1). It was very rocky and an average three feet to bedrock. The slope was 10-15%. Prior to applying treatments the pH was 5.6 and the soil was low in all major nutrients.

The original sward was totally lacking in legumes or productive grasses. It was dominated by field brome and broadleaf weeds.

The experimental design was a split block with establishment methods
(conventional and sod seeding) as main plots and with forage mixtures
(alfalfa-orchardgrass and birdsfoot trefoil-timothy) as subplots.

Conventionally seeded plots were plowed in August, 1976. Dolomitic
lime at two tons/acre was applied and incorporated in August 1976. Phosphoru
and potassium at 150 lbs/acre each and boron at 3 lbs/acre were disced into
the seedbed in April, 1977. No herbicide was used.

Plots to be sod-seeded received the same amounts of lime and fertilizer
and on the same dates as conventionally seeded plots; however, all materials
were left on the surface. Paraquat at one quart/acre with 1% v/v surfactant
was applied May 7, two days after seeding. No nitrogen was applied to any
of the plots before seeding or during the course of the experiment.

Alfalfa establishment

This experiment was on Site No. 3, a Charlton fine sandy loam, which is
deep and well drained and potentially one of the most productive upland
soils in New Hampshire (Table 1). The sod was dominated by quackgrass, with
minor amounts of dandelion and milkweed present.

In the fall of 1976, dolomitic lime at two tons/acre was applied to the
entire experimental area. Dandelions were treated with 2,4-D at one lb.
a.e./acre on April 21, 1977. Solubor[1] was applied to the entire area, pro-
viding 3 lbs. B/acre on April 22 and 150 lbs. each of P_2O_5 and K_2O was applie
overall on April 15.

The experiment was a split-block, in which establishment methods com-
prised the main plots. Subplots in one direction were dates of seeding
(May 5, May 16, and June 4, 1977) and subplots in the other direction were

herbicide treatments. Herbicide treatments consisted of glyphosate applied May 2 or May 16 at two quarts/acre for both establishment methods, EPTC (Eptam[1]) at four lbs/acre for conventional and paraquat at 0.50 lbs/acre for sod seeding. EPTC was sprayed on·the soil surface one day before seeding and immediately incorporated by discing. Paraquat was applied to the sod between two and five days after seeding. There were also untreated controls with each establishment method.

Evaluation and harvesting methods

Seedlings were counted within one month following seeding on randomly chosen areas of all plots. Initial harvest of spring seedings was 9-10 weeks following seeding for alfalfa, alfalfa mixtures, and red clover and 11-12 weeks for birdsfoot trefoil mixtures. Plots at Site 1 were harvested initially on June 14 and August 3, 1977, for fall and spring seedings, respectively.

Just prior to harvesting, plots were visually judged by three independent observers for botanical composition of harvested forage. In addition, samples were taken for hand separation of forage from Site 2. A flail-type harvester was used to determine forage yields. Approximately 1-lb sub-samples were taken for determining dry matter content of harvested forage and for determining quality factors.

Rainfall and temperature data for the period of the experiments, com-pared to 15-year means, are shown in Table 2.

Table 2. Monthly rainfall totals and temperature means for the growing
seasons 1977-82 at Durham, N.H. (1).

	Rainfall, inches						
	45-year[1] mean	1977[2]	1978	1979	1980	1981	1982
April	3.74	4.11	2.72	3.31	5.27	3.25	3.32
May	3.34	2.39	6.21	5.14	0.23	2.26	2.96
June	3.24	4.11	1.56	1.22	3.16	3.16	7.99
July	3.29	1.63	1.07	2.69	2.51	6.53	2.87
August	2.99	2.27	3.02	6.54	4.08	2.38	1.81
September	3.46	5.16	0.22	3.06	2.16	3.33	1.73
Total, June-July	6.53	5.74	2.63	3.91	5.67	9.69	10.86
Total, Apr.-Sept.	20.06	19.67	14.80	21.96	17.41	20.91	20.68

	Temperature, °F						
	45-year mean	1977[3]	1978	1979	1980	1981	1982
April	44.9	46.2	42.9	43.1	45.8	48.0	43.0
May	55.5	61.7	59.9	56.8	56.9	56.6	54.9
June	64.9	62.5	65.8	63.0	60.9	66.5	59.0
July	70.2	69.3	68.8	70.6	68.9	70.3	68.8
August	68.3	68.8	68.3	67.3	70.2	67.5	64.8
September	60.8	60.8	60.9	59.1	59.7	59.7	59.9
April-Sept.	60.8	61.6	61.1	60.0	60.4	61.4	58.4

[1]Based on mean of period 1931-75.

[2]Total for the month.

[3]Mean for the month.

RESULTS AND DISCUSSION

Red clover-timothy establishment

Results of August and May seedings are shown in Table 3. The August
seeding of red clover emerged within one week with at least 30 seedlings/
ft^2 in conventionally and sod-seeded plots. Seedlings on conventional plots lacked vigor and attained a height of only 2-3 inches in
the fall, while seedlings on sod-seeded plots were more vigorous. The
poorer vigor on conventional seedings might be attributed to the drying of
the seedbed as a result of repeated tillage in July and August, although
the repeated tillage was necessary to control quackgrass. There was a light
shower after seeding which encouraged germination, but failed to sustain
subsequent growth. On the other hand, killing the sod with herbicide pre-
vented use of soil moisture by the vegetation and left a mulch to further
conserve the limited rainfall which occurred following seeding.

The following spring there was an average of only four red clover
seedlings per ft^2 on conventional seedings; therefore, plots were reseeded
in May. Heaving of clover plants was very severe on the conventionally
seeded plots, which had a relatively bare soil surface, while clover seeded
into suppressed sod suffered little heaving injury.

Comparing May conventional and sod seedings, there was a tendency for
sod seedings to have fewer seedlings (Table 3). Recovery of sod following
paraquat application in May, compared with August treatment, was more rapid
and the vigorous growth of the cool-season grasses in May could have been a
factor. While there was less perennial grass competition with the conventional

Table 3. Effect of seeding method and pronamide on red clover seedling density and botanical composition of forage. Means are averaged over four fertility levels and four replications.

Seeding method	Seeding date	Pronamide rate[a]	Red clover Seedling density[b]	1977 Botanical composition[c]			1978 Botanical composition[c]		
				Legume	Grass	Broadleaf weeds	Legume	Grass	Broadleaf weeds
		lbs a.i./A	no./ft²	– – – – – – – – % – – – – – – – –					
Unseeded control	---	0	--	31	55	14	14	70	16
		3.0	--	61	27	12	13	68	19
Sod seeding	August	0	20	57	40	3	31	60	9
		3.0	27	83	16	1	23	60	17
Sod seeding	May	0	28	61	38	1	28	65	7
		3.0	33	71	27	2	34	62	4
Conventional	May	0	44	57	34	9	26	65	9
		3.0	50	69	9	22	28	40	32
		LSD .05	14	17	8	5	12	15	10

[a] Pronamide was applied in November 1977 (postemergent to August and preemergent to May seedings).

[b] Seedlings were counted April 19 and June 12 for August and May seedings, respectively. Conventional seeding in August averaged four red clover seedlings/ft² and plots were reseeded.

[c] Weighted average of three harvests in 1977 for August seedings and unseeded controls and two harvests for May seedings; weighted average of two harvests in 1978 for all treatments.

seeding, there were more annual weeds in the initial harvest than with sod seeding.

Pronamide improved red clover seedling density, whether applied post-emergent to the August seeding or preemergent to the May seeding. The effect of pronamide treatment in the fall was to delay quackgrass emergence in the spring so that red clover established in August was able to dominate the stand. In early May there was little growth of quackgrass on plots treated with pronamide and the effectiveness of paraquat was limited as a result. Perhaps a more effective control of quackgrass would have been to delay paraquat treatment until quackgrass was well emerged; however, seeding would have had to be delayed until late May.

Compared to unseeded controls, pronamide alone doubled the contribution of legumes, but the effect did not continue into the following year. Introduction of seed, in addition to pronamide treatment, further increased legume content of the forage. The combination of tillage and pronamide, as in the conventional seeding in May, nearly eliminated quackgrass, but allowed considerable annual weeds. Although legumes declined the year following establishment, seeded plots contained at least twice as much legume as unseeded controls. Grasses and broadleaf weeds accounted for a larger proportion of forage in the second year.

Compared with unseeded controls, forage yields increased an average of 68% and protein yields increased an average 83% the first year of production as a result of sod seeding in August (Table 4). Stands from sod seeding in August were more productive the initial year than those from either sod seeding or conventional seeding in May, which did not differ in forage

Table 4. Forage and protein yields of sod and conventional seedings,
          with and without pronamide, compared to unseeded controls.
          Means are averaged over four fertility levels and four
          replications.

Seeding method	Seeding date	Pronamide rate	1977 Yield		1978 Yield	
			Forage	Protein	Forage	Protein
		lbs/Acre	- - - - - Tons/Acre - - - - - -			
Unseeded control	--	0	2.22	0.30	2.28	0.26
		3.0	1.82	0.31	2.16	0.26
Sod seeding	August	0	3.39	0.52	2.13	0.30
		3.0	3.37	0.58	2.00	0.26
Sod seeding	May	0	1.89	0.28	2.35	0.30
		3.0	1.96	0.29	2.20	0.32
Conventional	May	0	1.81	0.30	2.20	0.27
		3.0	1.73	0.29	1.82	0.24
		LSD .05	0.76	0.22	0.70	0.13

or protein yield. Forage yields of May seedings were slightly lower than

unseeded controls, since considerable yield was sacrificed by suppressing the

sod in the spring prior to seeding or, in the case of conventional seeding,

having killed the sod.

Protein percentage of harvested forage (data not shown), improved with

the use of pronamide, as expected from the increase in legume composition

of the sward. Pronamide application did not increase forage yields, indicati

that clover merely replaced the grass which pronamide eliminated.

In terms of red clover seedling density and legume content of forage
the first year of production, 250-500 lbs/acre of 5-20-20 applied before
seeding was optimum (Table 5). The decline in legume component with the
higher rate of fertilizer (1000 lbs/acre) was greater with sod seeding than
with conventional seeding. The higher fertilization rates, because of the
higher nitrogen, increased growth of recovering grasses in the sod-seeded
plots. In conventionally seeded plots there was little grass to stimulate.
It is not known whether comparable levels of 0-20-20 might have produced different results, but the practice of applying 500 lbs/acre or more of 5-20-20,
a common recommendation with conventional seedings, would not be advised
with sod seedings since nitrogen favors grass growth and results in excessive
competition with legume seedlings.

Establishment of legume-grass mixtures

Comparative results of seeding method and forage mixtures are shown in
Table 6. Seedling density was between 20 and 30 legume plants/ft^2 on all
plots one month following seeding (data not shown). Soil moisture was adequate
for seedling development. During the first two months following seeding more
rapid growth and development of seedlings occurred with conventional, compared
with sod seeding, with legumes compared with grasses, and with alfalfa compared with birdsfoot trefoil. For example, the first harvest, which represented similar amounts of legume growth on conventional plots was on July 15
and August 6 for the alfalfa-orchardgrass and birdsfoot trefoil-timothy
mixtures, respectively. Although the mixtures did not differ in yield the

Table 5. Effect of fertility level on red clover seedling density and botanical composition of forage.

Seeding method	Seeding date	Rate of 5-20-20	Red clover Seedling density	[a]Botanical composition, 1977			1977 Yield
		lbs/acre	no./ft²	Legume	Grass	Broadleaf weeds	b ns/acre
				- - -	%	- - -	
Unseeded control	--	0	--	50	40	10	2.17
		250	--	55	39	6	2.09
		500	--	46	47	7	1.99
		1000	--	47	46	7	2.19
Sod seeding	August	0	27	74	24	2	3.15
		250	34	75	25	0	3.40
		500	29	72	27	1	3.52
		1000	15	60	40	0	3.49
Sod seeding	May	0	34	67	32	1	1.70
		250	41	67	33	0	1.91
		500	36	64	30	0	1.94
		100	25	63	25	2	2.01
Conventional	May	0	45	74	21	5	1.51
		250	48	75	21	4	1.92
		500	51	75	17	8	1.86
		1000	45	73	17	10	1.92
		LSD .05	12	19	14	4	0.81

[a]Weighted average of three harvests in 1977 for August seedings and unseeded controls and two harvests for May seedings; weighted average of two harvests in 1978 for all treatments.

year of establishment (Table 6), the slower growth from sod seeding resulted in about 30% lower yields than conventional seedings.

In 1978 rainfall was about average in May, but considerably below average in June and July (Table 2). There was only 1.78 inch of rainfall from June 10 to August 1, with the greatest amount of only 0.52 inch. Seasonal yields were affected to the extent that slightly over half of total forage yield was harvested on June 2. The total of July 11 and August 22 harvests was less than half of the seasonal yield.

There was an interaction in 1978 seasonal yield in that with sod seeding alfalfa-orchardgrass yielded somewhat lower than birdsfoot trefoil-timothy; however, the difference in forage mixtures was not significant with conventional seeding (Table 6). The lower yield of alfalfa-orchardgrass with sod seeding may have resulted from the lack of pH adjustment through the plow layer, since lime was not incorporated and is noted for slow downward movement. Birdsfoot trefoil is somewhat more tolerant of acidity and may have benefitted by way of moisture conservation with sod seeding, in which a mulch is left intact. Regrowth of birdsfoot trefoil-timothy following the first harvest was about 20% higher on sod-seeded, compared with conventionally-seeded treatments (data not shown).

In 1979 the largest rainfall in June and the first half of July was 0.39 inch. The yield distribution was similar to that in 1978. Birdsfoot trefoil-timothy yielded better with sod seeding than with conventional seeding. Yields were similar at the first harvest, but some 15% higher in favor of sod seeding, with summer regrowth. Alfalfa-orchardgrass produced higher yields on sod-seeded plots than in 1978.

Forage yields were higher in 1980 and 1981 than in the previous two years because of greater and more evenly distributed rainfall over the growing season. There were no significant differences due to method of establishment or forage mixture. In contrast to the two previous years, about 60% of the seasonal forage yield occurred with regrowth following the first harvest.

Table 6. Seasonal forage yields[a] and six-year total yields of two mixtures seeded directly into sod and conventionally in May, 1977.

Establishment method	Forage mixture	Forage yield, by year						Total forage yield, 6 years
		1977	1978	1979	1980	1981	1982	
		- - - -	- - -	- - -	tons/acre	- - -	- - -	- - - - -
Sod seeding								
	Alfalfa-orchardgrass	1.30b	2.51b	3.12a	3.36a	3.19a	3.44a	16.92
	B. trefoil-timothy	1.31b	3.04a	3.09a	3.39a	3.05a	2.90b	16.78
Conventional								
	Alfalfa-orchardgrass	1.87a	2.72ab	3.06a	3.32a	3.22a	3.57a	17.76
	B. trefoil-timothy	1.82a	2.84ab	2.79b	3.12a	2.97a	2.91b	16.45

[a]Means in a column followed by the same letter are not significantly different according to Dunan's New Multiple Range Test.

Although rainfall in 1982 was well above average, the average temperature was considerably below the 45-year average. Seasonal yields of alfalfa-orchardgrass were significantly greater than those of birdsfoot trefoil-timothy. Average yields over the six-year duration of the stands were similar for sod seeding and conventional seeding.

In the establishment year legume content of harvested forage was lower with mixtures seeded directly into sod, compared with conventional seedings (Table 7). Correspondingly, protein content of harvested forage was lower following sod seeding. The difference was greatest with the alfalfa-orchardgrass mixture. There was a greater amount of annual broadleaf weeds with conventional seeding in the year of establishment and, while they did not seem to have a negative impact on protein content of forage, they may have affected feeding value.

Average protein content of forage increased in the year following seeding as legumes dominated stands to a greater extent. Alfalfa dominated to a greater degree than birdsfoot trefoil through the course of the experiment. Although the legume proportion of harvested forage declined somewhat in years five and six, there were still acceptable stands of both mixtures with both establishment methods.

Alfalfa establishment

May 5 seeding. There was ample rainfall the week following the seeding, resulting in good germination and emergence of alfalfa. Seedling density two weeks after seeding was lowest with alfalfa seeded directly into quack-

Table 7. Legume and protein content[a] of forage harvested over a six-year period following establishment of two mixtures by conventional and sod seeding.

Establishment method	Forage mixture	1977	1978	1979	1980	1981	1982
				Legume content, %			
Sod seeding	Alfalfa-orchardgrass	32c	54a	61a	58a	55a	50a
	Birdsfoot trefoil-timothy	32c	61a	51ab	53ab	51a	41ab
Conventional	Alfalfa-orchardgrass	69a	60a	68a	64a	56a	49a
	Birdsfoot trefoil-timothy	43b	66a	45b	46b	43b	32b
				Protein content, %			
Sod seeding	Alfalfa-orchardgrass	13.7b	15.1b	15.6a	14.9ab	15.0a	14.5a
	Birdsfoot trefoil-timothy	9.8c	16.5ab	15.3a	16.1a	15.4a	13.6b
Conventional	Alfalfa-orchardgrass	17.0a	16.5ab	16.4a	15.2ab	15.3a	14.2a
	Birdsfoot trefoil-timothy	10.3d	17.3a	14.9a	14.6b	14.6a	13.2b

[a]Means are weighted averages, based on relative yields of multiple harvests each year. Means within columns and quality evaluation with the same letter are not significantly different according to Duncan's New Multiple Range Test.

grass sod without herbicide treatment (Table 8). Control of quackgrass with
either glyphosate or paraquat before seeding into the sod resulted in
greater numbers of alfalfa seedlings than did conventional seeding.

In the seeding year yields were generally lower with sod seeding than
with conventional seeding. The difference was greatest with no herbicide,
in which almost no alfalfa was established with sod seeding. Where glyphosate
was applied prior to seeding, alfalfa established well with sod seeding, but
yields were still about 20% less than with conventional seeding. The lower
yields with sod seeding were the result of slower development and less vigor
of alfalfa seedlings, especially until the first harvest (July 11).

The differences in yield between sod and conventional seedings largely
disappeared the year after seeding, except in untreated plots. There was
considerable improvement in total forage and alfalfa yields in plots
originally treated with paraquat at seeding. With conventional seeding,
alfalfa established successfully and was able to dominate in the second
year, whereas with sod seedings and no herbicide application quackgrass
was still dominant in the second year.

May 21 seeding. In contrast to the May 5 seeding, there was no rainfall
for 10 days following the May 21 seeding. Yields for the season were, on
average, 12% lower than seedings on May 5 (Tables 8 and 9). As with the
earlier seeding date, sod seeding resulted in about 20% lower forage yield
than conventional seeding. By the end of the first season alfalfa represented over 90% of the harvested forage from plots treated with glyphosate.

Table 8. Yields[a] of forage and alfalfa following May 5 conventional and sod seedings of alfalfa into a heavily quackgrass-infested field.

Seeding method and herbicide treatment	Alfalfa seedling density	Seeding year yields		Second year yields	
		Total forage	Alfalfa component	Total forage	Alfalfa component
	no./ft^2	- - - - - - - - - tons/acre - - - - - - - - -			
Conventional seeding					
Untreated	19	2.8	1.4	4.4	4.1
EPTC	16	2.6	1.7	4.7	4.6
Glyphosate (May 2)	18	3.1	2.6	4.3	4.1
Sod seeding					
Untreated	11	1.9	0.1	2.1	0.8
Paraquat	27	2.4	0.8	4.2	3.7
Glyphosate (May 2)	24	2.5	2.2	4.3	4.2
LSD .05 between seeding methods		0.5	0.6	0.9	1.1
LSD .05 within seeding methods		0.4	0.5	0.7	0.8

[a]Yields the seeding year are sums of July 11 and August 31, 1977 harvests; yields the second year are sums of May 29, July 10, and August 18, 1978 harvests.

Table 9. Yields[a] of forage and alfalfa following May 21 conventional and sod seedings of alfalfa into a heavily quackgrass-infested field.

Seeding method and herbicide treatment	Alfalfa seedling density	Seeding year yields		Second year yields	
		Total forage	Alfalfa component	Total forage	Alfalfa component
	no./ft^2	- - - - - - - - tons/acre - - - - - - - -			
Conventional seeding					
Untreated	17	2.1	0.4	3.5	2.6
EPTC	21	2.3	0.9	3.9	3.4
Glyphosate (May 16)	20	2.3	1.4	4.0	3.8
Sod seeding					
Untreated	14	1.3	0.03	2.3	0.8
Paraquat	16	1.8	0.1	2.5	1.1
Glyphosate (May 16)	14	1.8	1.1	4.0	3.7
LSD .05 between seeding methods	0.5	0.6	0.9	1.1	
LSD .05 within seeding methods	0.4	0.5	0.7	0.8	

[a]Yields the seeding year are sums of July 24 and August 31, 1977; yields the second year are sums of May 29, July 10, and August 18, 1978 harvests.

Quackgrass was not so well controlled with other herbicides and represented a larger proportion of harvested forage. Sod seeding with paraquat treatment resulted in forage the seeding year containing only 5% alfalfa, yet alfalfa represented 44% of harvested. forage the following year. As with the earlier seeding, herbicide treatment was relatively more important for sod seeding than for conventional seeding.

June 4 seeding . Yield data are shown in Table 10. The average reduction in seeding year yield, compared with the May 2 seeding, was 37%. As with the May seeding, there was a lower yield with sod seeding than with conventional seeding in the seeding year.

Although only 13 alfalfa seedlings/ft^2 were established with sod seeding following glyphosate application (compared with 29 seedlings/ft^2 with the same treatment and conventional seeding), alfalfa dominated the stand and produced yields similar to those of the conventional seedings in the year following seeding. The conditions that apparently contributed to the successful establishment by sod seeding with glyphosate were excellent control of quackgrass, good moisture conservation by retaining surface mulch, and few annual weeds. There were fewer annual weeds invading sod-seeded than conventional seedings.

Table 10. Yields[a] of forage and alfalfa following June 4 conventional and sod seedings of alfalfa into a heavily quackgrass-infested field.

Seeding method and herbicide treatment	Alfalfa seedling density	Seeding year yields		Second year yields	
		Total forage	Alfalfa component	Total forage	Alfalfa component
	no./ft^2	- - - - - - -		tons/acre - - - - - - -	
Conventional seeding					
Untreated	23	1.5	0.8	3.9	3.5
EPTC	26	2.0	1.7	4.3	4.1
Glyphosate (May 16)	29	1.6	1.5	4.2	4.0
Sod seeding					
Untreated	10	1.5	0.0	b	b
Paraquat	16	1.7	0.1	2.4	1.3
Glyphosate (May 16)	13	1.4	1.1	4.0	3.7
LSD .05 between seeding methods		0.5	0.6	0.9	1.1
LSD .05 within seeding methods		0.4	0.5	0.7	0.8

[a]Yields the seeding year are sums of August 8 and October 21, 1977 harvests; yields the second year are sums of May 29, July 10, and August 18, 1978 harvests.

[b]Plots not harvested in 1978.

CONCLUSIONS

Based on the results of these experiments, the following conclusions were made:

1. Legumes were established successfully in sods without the usual tillage preparatory steps and without nitrogen fertilizer.

2. Except on a seasonally wet site, sod seedings were slower to establish and yields in the seeding year were 15-25% lower than with conventional seedings. Yields in succeeding years were equivalent for both methods of establishment.

3. Red clover seeded in August directly into sod on a seasonally wet soil overwintered successfully, while stands seeded conventionally failed to overwinter due to heaving. On the same soil, sod seeding in August resulted in greater improvement in forage and red clover yields, relative to unseeded controls, than sod or conventional seedings in May.

4. Renovation by sod seeding on three sites and four different dates improved forage and protein yields considerably, compared with unseeded controls. Conventional renovation, in the same studies, also improved yields over controls, except at one site where the seeding failed.

5. With aggressive species such as quackgrass, herbicide application was much more important for sod seeding than for conventional seeding. Best establishment of alfalfa into quackgrass sod without tillage resulted when quackgrass was killed prior to seeding.

6. Since the soil surface was disturbed minimally, there was little germination of annual weeds subsequent to sod seedings; annual weeds were much more common in conventional seedings.

7. As with conventional seeding, stands were denser and yields higher with seeding early in May, compared with mid-May or early June.

REFERENCES

1. Byers, G.L., and D.L. Goodrich. 1977. Selected climates of New Hampshire. N.H. Agr. Exp. Sta. Res. Report No. 60.

2. Cullen, N.A. 1970. The effect of grazing, time of sowing, fertilizer, and paraquat on the germination and survival of oversown grasses and clovers. Proc. XI Inter. Grassl. Congr. pp. 112-115.

3. Decker, A.M., H.J. Retzer, and F.G. Swain. 1964. Improved soil openers for the establishment of small seeded legumes in sod. Agron. J. 56:211-214.

4. Decker, A.M., H.J. Retzer, M.L. Sarna, and H.D. Kerr. 1969. Permanent pastures improved with sod-seeding and fertilization. Agron. J. 61:243-247.

5. Kolega, J.J., and R.S. Palmer. 1961. Temperature guide for New England. N.H. Agr. Exp. Sta. Tech. Bull. 105.

6. Linscott, D.C. 1979. Projections for no-tillage forage systems for the Northeast. NE Amer. Soc. Agron. Abstr., pp. 10-12.

7. Mueller-Warrant, G.W., and D.W. Koch. 1979. Chemical control of orchardgrass preceding a no-till alfalfa seeding. Proc. NE Weed Sci. Soc. 33:31-32.

8. Mueller-Warrant, G.W., and D.W. Koch. 1980. Establishment of alfalfa by conventional and minimum-tillage seeding techniques in a quackgrass-dominant sward. Agron. J. 72:884-889.

9. Newman, R.J. 1966. Problems of grassland establishment and maintenance on hill-country in Victoria. Proc. X Inter. Grassl. Congr., pp. 875-878.

10. Sprague, M.A. 1952. The substitution of chemicals for tillage in pasture renovation. Agron. J. 44:405-409.

11. Sprague, M.A. 1960. Seedbed preparation and improvement of unplowable pastures using herbicides. Proc. VIII Inter. Grassl. Congr. pp. 264-266.

12. Taylor, T.H., E.M. Smith, and W.C. Templeton, Jr. 1969. Use of minimum tillage and herbicide for establishing legumes in Kentucky bluegrass (Poa pratensis L.) swards. Agron. J. 61:761-766.

13. Triplett, G.B., Jr., R.W. Van Keuren, and V.H. Watson. 1975. The role of herbicides in pasture renovation. In Proc. of No Tillage Forage Symposium. The Ohio State University.

14. Van Keuren, R.W., and G.B. Triplett. 1970. Seeding legumes into established grass swards. Proc. XI Inter. Grassl. Congr., pp. 131-134.

15. Warboys, I.B. 1966. Improvement of permanent pasture by overdrilling and oversowing. Exp. Agric. 3:63-72.

16. Wedin, W.R., J.D. Donker, and G.C. Martin. 1965. An evaluation of nitrogen fertilization in legume-grass and all-grass pastures. Agron. J. 57:185-188.

17. White, J.G.H. 1970. Establishment of lucerne (Medicago sativa L.) in uncultivated country by sod seeding and overseeding. Proc. XI Inter. Grassl. Congr., pp. 134-138.

Lightning Source UK Ltd.
Milton Keynes UK
UKHW041152150219
337137UK00013B/1564/P